THE LITTLE GUIDE TO

CHRISTIAN LOUBOUTIN

First published in 2026 by OH
An Imprint of HEADLINE PUBLISHING GROUP LIMITED

1

Disclaimer:
This book has not been licensed, approved, sponsored, or endorsed by Christian Louboutin or any rightsholder(s) in respect of this brand.

Christian Louboutin is a registerd trademark owned by CLERMON ET ASSOCIES
83 Rue de Tocqueville, Paris, 75017, France

Cataloguing in Publication Data is available from the British Library

ISBN: 978-1-03543-344-5

Compiled and written by Katie Meegan
Editorial: Phoebe Hills
Designed and typeset in Avenir by Stephen Cary
Project manager: Russell Porter
Production: Arlene Lestrade
Printed and bound in Dubai

Headline's policy is to use papers that are natural, renewable and recyclable products and made from wood grown in well-managed forests and other controlled sources. The logging and manufacturing processes are expected to conform to the environmental regulations of the country of origin.

HEADLINE PUBLISHING GROUP LIMITED
An Hachette UK Company
Carmelite House, 50 Victoria Embankment, London EC4Y 0DZ

The authorised representative in the EEA is Hachette Ireland, 8 Castlecourt Centre, Dublin 15, D15 XTP3, Ireland (email: info@hbgi.ie)

www.headline.co.uk www.hachette.co.uk

THE LITTLE GUIDE TO

CHRISTIAN LOUBOUTIN

STYLE TO LIVE BY

Unofficial and Unauthorized

CONTENTS

INTRODUCTION

Christian Louboutin didn't simply design shoes – he revolutionized the world of luxury footwear. Born in Paris's multi-cultural 12th arrondissement, Louboutin charted an extraordinary path from a school dropout to one of the most influential figures in modern luxury. What began as a teenage fascination with the forbidden blossomed into a career shaped by stints at legendary fashion houses like Roger Vivier and Yves Saint Laurent, culminating in the creation of a brand that has become a global symbol of elegance and audacity. His story is one of creativity, boldness and an enduring passion for beauty. For Louboutin, high heels are far more than accessories – they are instruments of empowerment and desire.

Famed for fusing fantasy with meticulous craftsmanship, Louboutin has redefined how we view shoes. His designs are theatrical, sensual and unapologetically bold, turning every red sole into a statement of identity and self-expression. Yet beyond the glitz and glamour lies a deeply personal artistic vision, inspired by his love of travel, cabaret, architecture and the female form. Despite his indisputable commercial and artistic success, Louboutin has faced his share of critics: from those that claim his shoes are anti-feminist to those that would try to copy them. Louboutin has consistently stood firm in his belief that his shoes empower women – and as for the imitators, one need only look to his triumphant court battle against Yves Saint Laurent...

From fashion runways and red carpets to the lyrics of hip-hop anthems and the pages of Vogue, Louboutins have embedded themselves into pop culture, surpassing trends to become timelessly iconic. The red sole has become more than a signature design – it is a signal of status, seduction and unmistakable style.

So step into the glamorous world of Christian Louboutin – where craftsmanship meets fantasy, and every shoe tells a story.

CHAPTER ONE

SOLE PURPOSE

BORN IN PARIS'S LIVELY 12TH ARRONDISSEMENT, CHRISTIAN LOUBOUTIN GREW UP SURROUNDED BY A VIBRANT MIX OF CULTURES AND CREATIVITY.

AFTER LEAVING HOME AT JUST TWELVE YEARS OLD, HE QUICKLY BECAME IMMERSED IN THE CITY'S ELECTRIC NIGHTLIFE – A WORLD OF GLAMOUR AND REBELLION THAT WOULD GO ON TO SHAPE HIS BOLD, THEATRICAL DESIGNS FOR DECADES TO COME.

My working-class parents were from Brittany. I had a great childhood but liked escaping routine. I was often absent from school, and expelled.

”

Christian Louboutin

On his true childhood and routine,
BBC, March 2, 2020

Christian Louboutin was born on January 7, 1964, in Paris's 12th arrondissement.

He was the only son in a family of three daughters.

When you are a child, adults, especially teachers, are always asking you, 'What do you want to be when you grow up?' I was pretty lazy and got so bored with this question I made up an answer, 'A shoe designer.'

”

Christian Louboutin

On answering a childhood question and ultimately carving the path for his career, *Vintage Shoes: Collecting Wearing Vintage Classics*, Caroline Cox, 2022

She was a free spirit, never judging, the best support. When you have this education, driven by love, it keeps you straight for a long time – and when you have a solid character, you can do anything.

”

Christian Louboutin

On the influence of his mother, *Independent*, May 26, 2012

Louboutin's mother was a homemaker from Brittany and his father was a cabinetmaker, whose meticulous craftsmanship left a lasting impression.

It was from him that Louboutin learned the value of working with his hands – a skill that would later define his approach to shoemaking.

He showed me a piece of wood and said, 'You see, there is a line. If you go in the direction of the grain, you can do beautiful sculptures. If you go against, it never works: You end up having splinters.' I took it literally, but also as a metaphor – go in the direction of the grain of life and good things happen to you; go against it, and you end up breaking yourself and everything around you.

Christian Louboutin

Recalling the advice that his father, a cabinetmaker, once gave him, *Independent*, May 26, 2012

I was born in the 12th arrondissement and have always had a close and special connection with the Palais de la Porte Dorée. As a child, I went there during weekends for the Tropical Aquarium... and then began to explore the place, which at that time also housed Musée des Arts Africains et Océaniens.

”

Christian Louboutin

On the cultural institutions that influenced his early creativity, *Elle Decoration*, April 9, 2020

School never captured Louboutin's interest – he was expelled three times before leaving both the classroom and his home behind at the tender age of twelve.

Throughout his teen years, he immersed himself in punk culture – a movement that continues to influence his work to this day.

I never had a conflict; I was just quite mature. I left, but came back for lunch; left, came back another day to sleep in my old bedroom. When I was 15, I came back for a few months, and then left. It never was a break. It was much more natural; the progression of it.

”

Christian Louboutin

On leaving home at twelve years old, *Independent*, May 26, 2012

I never was that close. I have 23 years difference with my oldest sister, and I'm 16 years younger than my second sister.

Christian Louboutin

On his distant relationship with his elder sisters, *Independent*, May 26, 2012

My long-time love of the French showgirl and stage performers means I design a lot of very high heels that lengthen the leg and work best when in movement and combine a lot of elements of fantasy.

Christian Louboutin

On his first job working backstage at a Parisian cabaret – an experience that continued to shape his work in the coming decades, *Vintage Shoes: Collecting Wearing Vintage Classics*, Caroline Cox, 2022

Behind that moment of beauty there is someone who probably suffers for hours and hours.

Christian Louboutin

On being drawn to artists and performers, and the dedication to their craft, *10 Magazine*, December 15, 2021

[When] I was a kid, I realized I was more of an actor than a spectator. When I was going to clubs as a teenager in the 70s, I would dance. I would not stare at people doing something. I would do something.

Christian Louboutin

On being a performer rather than an observer during his party-filled youth, *10 Magazine*, December 15, 2021

A fixture of the Parisian punk and party scene, Louboutin briefly pursued an acting career, starring in two films: The 1979 cult classic *Race d'ep* and *The Homosexual Century*.

He worked behind the scenes at a cabaret, where his fascination with footwear first took hold – designing shoes for the dancers and laying the foundations for his future in fashion.

There's a generosity in being bold and beautiful, because you only give the good sides to people. You know, you may suffer, but that is not what you're delivering as a message.

”

Christian Louboutin

On performance and artistry being a means to share the best of yourself with others, *10 Magazine*, December 15, 2021

Looking back, French punk was ultra-glam, not at all dark – we wore huge safety-pin bracelets, we never went for piercings.

Christian Louboutin

On the French punk aesthetic that he was immersed in, BBC, March 2, 2020

[Louboutin] got himself noticed on the fashion scene becoming part of the 'Bande de Bandeau' or the 'Headband Gang'

Darla-Jane Gilroy

Fashion historian, on Louboutin's wild youth, *Little Book of Christian Louboutin: The story of the iconic shoe designer*, Darla-Jane Gilroy, 2021

The studs on my shoes aren't about fetishism, they reference punk style.

Christian Louboutin

On the influence of punk style in his designs, BBC, March 2, 2020

Louboutin traces his earliest fascination with shoes back to 1976, during a visit to an exhibition at the Musée National des Arts d'Afrique et d'Océanie. He noticed a sign forbidding women from wearing heels to protect the delicate flooring.

This sparked rebellion within him, and it was then that he vowed to create heels that empowered women instead of limiting them.

It was a high-heel shoe covered in a big red cross, as stilettos were forbidden… It was a typical style shoe from the 1950s, but… I had never seen something like that as a child. It made me understand you can create anything with a sketch, and that's how I started to draw shoes.

”

Christian Louboutin

On the moment he discovered the power of high heels, ten-membership.com, March 5, 2021

It was intriguing, full of masks and jewellery. Most of Paris's major museums are in the west of the city. This one is a hidden gem in the east.

Christian Louboutin

On the museums of Paris and their intrigue, BBC, March 2, 2020

I was fascinated by the Egyptian and Bollywood movies they screened.

”

Christian Louboutin

On the cultural influences that he discovered at the cinema during his younger years, BBC, March 2, 2020

In his youth, Louboutin travelled widely, with India and Egypt leaving a lasting impression on him creatively.

Years later, his sister revealed a family secret: Louboutin's biological father was, in fact, an Egyptian man with whom his mother had once had a secret affair.

For Louboutin – who had always felt different from the rest of his family – the news was a revelation.

It's funny, I fantasized as a child that I'd been adopted, as I was darker skinned than my three blonde sisters. So, it was a nice surprise.

”

Christian Louboutin

On his Egyptian heritage and feeling different from his siblings, BBC, March 2, 2020

Travelling means a lot to me; it embodies independence but also the respect of others.

”

Christian Louboutin

On leading a rather nomadic existence in his teens and early twenties, ten-membership.com, March 5, 2021

I am one of those people who believes travel is essential for tolerance, intelligence and discovery. Some things need to be seen, smelled, heard, lived to understand the beauty of it. That's why I live to travel.

”

Christian Louboutin

On the significance of travelling, ten-membership.com, March 5, 2021

The inspirations from my youth are perennial.

”

Christian Louboutin

On the lasting influences of his youth, BBC, March 2, 2020

It was the night club. It was the first time in Paris that people were super dressing up. The music was great. We were this band of super-young people, in all our best clothes.

”

Christian Louboutin

On his youth in La Palace nightclub – Paris's equivalent to Studio 54, *The New Yorker*, March 21, 2011

Vivier's shoes spoke by themselves – he understood that a shoe has bone structure, and that bone structure has to be perfect.

Christian Louboutin

On taking inspiration from earlier shoe designer Roger Vivier, who was known for being a particular favourite of Marilyn Monroe, *Vintage Shoes: Collecting and Wearing Designer Classics*, Caroline Cox, 2022

Louboutin eventually returned to Paris with a portfolio of elaborate high heel sketches. Determined to break into the fashion world, he presented his designs to top couture houses and landed a job in the house of Charles Jourdan.

It was there that he met Roger Vivier – the legendary creator of the modern stiletto – and soon after Louboutin secured a traineeship in Vivier's atelier.

I started designing shoes but not for the fashion industry. My goal was never to work in the fashion industry in general. My thing was shoes. I see things changing, but apart from having more offices now than I did before, it doesn't really include me.

”

Christian Louboutin

On staying true to his real passion, *British Vogue*, April 5, 2018

When I started designing shoes, they were simply considered an accessory, but by the end of the 1990s, shoes had become an essential component of a woman's wardrobe and the expression of a feminine strength.

”

Christian Louboutin

On the changing importance of fashion footwear, ten-membership.com, March 5, 2021

Louboutin eventually branched out on his own as a freelance designer, creating shoes for luxury houses such as Yves Saint Laurent and Chanel.

But in the late 1980s, he took an unexpected detour from fashion, trading heels for hedges as he pursued a brief stint in landscape gardening. However, the pull of design proved too strong – he soon returned to the world of shoes.

I didn't last long: I missed my shoes.

Christian Louboutin

On his short career as a landscape designer, BBC, March 2, 2020

In 1991, Christian Louboutin opened the doors to his first boutique in Paris.

Among his earliest clients was Princess Caroline of Monaco – an endorsement that catapulted his fledging brand into the spotlight.

It wasn't long before Louboutin became the go-to shoe designer for the rich, famous and fashion obsessed – a cultural force whose red-soled legacy continues to stride confidently forward today.

Yes, I wanted to be a shoe designer, but I never thought it could be a profession. But what was the alternative? Doctor? Too dirty! Air hostess? Maybe not! Then someone gave me a book on Roger Vivier, and, *chérie*, instantly I knew that was it!

”

Christian Louboutin

On his true calling and discovering a career that matched his passion, newyorker.com, March 21, 2011

Galerie Véro-Dodat, rue Jean Jacques Rousseau

The address of the first Louboutin shop in Paris. Nestled within a preserved 19th-century arcade in the city's 1st arrondissement.

With its black-and-white tiled floors, gilded mirrors and neoclassical charm, Galerie Véro-Dodat offered the perfect backdrop for Louboutin's bold, theatrical designs.

I'm very fortunate because I was born with a lot of enthusiasm and huge energy.

”

Christian Louboutin

On his inherent passion, *10 Magazine*, December 15, 2021

CHAPTER TWO

KILLER HEELS

LOUBOUTIN IS SYNONYMOUS WITH GROUNDBREAKINGLY HIGH HEELS – BUT THERE'S MORE TO A SHARP STILETTO THAN MEETS THE EYE.

FROM HEEL TO TOE, EVERY PAIR IS A MASTERCLASS IN DESIGN AND ENGINEERING, WHERE BALANCE, STRUCTURE AND AESTHETICS CONVERGE IN PERFECT HARMONY.

FROM THE CURVE OF THE ARCH TO THE PLACEMENT OF THE HEEL TIP, EACH ELEMENT IS CAREFULLY CONSIDERED TO CREATE NOT ONLY BEAUTY BUT WEARABILITY – PROOF THAT A LOUBOUTIN HEEL IS AS MUCH A FEAT OF ARCHITECTURE AS IT IS A FASHION STATEMENT.

So the shoe is really the pedestal for… not the personality, but definitely the posture and the way you move and interpret your body.

Christian Louboutin

On the role the high heel has in shaping how a person carries themselves, *10 Magazine*, December 15, 2021

Dubbed the "King of the stiletto", Christian Louboutin is known for creating high heels that are as challenging to wear as they are stunning to behold – an intentional touch that adds an extra layer of exclusivity to each pair.

For Louboutin, shoes have never been about comfort; they are about elegance, allure and the art of seduction.

I don't think comfort equals happiness.

”

Christian Louboutin

On his shoes being uncomfortable to wear, an accusation often levelled against him, *Independent*, May 26, 2012

You are carrying your clothes, but you are carried by your shoes.

Christian Louboutin

On the importance of shoes in fashion and for posture, *10 Magazine*, December 15, 2021

I don't hate the idea of comfort. I just don't think it's important for me as a designer... Some people say, for instance, they're in a comfortable relationship. I favour someone who would tell me: 'I am in a very passionate relationship'...

It's the same thing for shoes. I would rather someone say, 'Your shoes look passionate and sexy' than 'Your shoes look so comfortable'.

”

Christian Louboutin

On favours shoes that are beautiful over comfortable, *Independent*, May 26, 2012

The shoe is the pedestal of your body, but also an introduction to your personality.

”

Christian Louboutin

On shoes being an expression of one's personality, ten-membership.com, March 5, 2021

Even if you don't necessarily like your body, most people like their feet. Let's say you have very skinny feet – it looks very elegant and pretty. If you have very round feet, they look like a baby's feet... The foot has this magic possibility to be transformed and transport people into another type of universe.

Christian Louboutin

On the versatility of feet and why they are his favourite part of the body to design for, *10 Magazine*, December 15, 2021

The foot has this lucky thing... Think of Greek statues. Look how many people love the foot of the baby! There is something super-charming about the baby foot.

99

Christian Louboutin

On the luckiness of feet, newyorker.com, March 21, 2011

The wellbeing [aspect] of looking good [is important] and helps a lot of people. You should have as much respect for those who are concerned by boldness and beauty as those who aren't. Bold and beautiful, for me, is a bit of a definition of freedom, too.

”

Christian Louboutin

Often linking his shoe designs with self-love and confidence, *10 Magazine*, December 15, 2021

When a woman buys a pair of shoes, she never looks at the shoe. She stands up and looks in the mirror, she looks at the breast, the ass, from the front, from the side… If she likes herself, then she considers the shoe.

”

Christian Louboutin

On being confident when buying shoes, newyorker.com, March 21, 2011

“

Stilettos remain a shorthand for glamorous femininity.

”

Lauren Cochrane

Fashion writer and historian, *The Ten: Stories Behind the Fashion Classics*, Lauren Cochrane, 2021

Each time a model is released for a new collection, I was the person who sketched it. Drawings are important, but in my work, the most important step is when the model tries on the prototype.

”

Christian Louboutin

On his designing process that has remained largely unchanged since he opened his first shop over thirty years ago, ten-membership.com, March 5, 2021

The largest personal collection of Louboutins belongs to American romance novelist Danielle Steel, who is said to own more than 6,000 pairs.

A devoted fan of the red sole, she is also known for buying up to 80 pairs in a single shopping spree – making her a true icon of Louboutin devotion.

It's saying women are not smart enough to make their own choices.

Christian Louboutin

On accustions of his shoes being anti-feminist, *Independent*, May 26, 2012

I'll do shoes for the lady who lunches, but it would be, like, a really nasty lunch, talking about men. But where I draw the line, what I absolutely won't do, is the lady who plays bridge in the afternoon.

”

Christian Louboutin

On his ideal client, newyorker.com, March 21, 2011

My earliest designs were more dressed-up, embellished. Now I tend to go for simpler, more bare designs, ones that emphasize the shape of the leg. I've gone from dressy to undressed.

Christian Louboutin

On the development of his design ethos, BBC, March 2, 2020

Throughout history, the stiletto heel has been linked to erotism and desire. With his towering heels, signature studs and bold detailing, Christian Louboutin has has often featured in this discussion.

But beyond aesthetics lies a deeper debate around the role of the stiletto in female empowerment.

Louboutin's answer is clear: his shoes empower the wearer, offering confidence, allure and a bold expression of self.

What I'm trying to do is eroticism, I'm not trying to do pornography.

Christian Louboutin

On the themes he aims to evoke through his shoes, "Christian Louboutin: The World's Most Luxurious Shoes", Channel 4, 2009

I appreciate that some perceive them that way. But people project their own ideas on to a designer's work, and sometimes this isn't what the designer intended.

Christian Louboutin

On critics having varying perceptions of his creations, BBC, March 2, 2020

Stilettos since the 60s have been about sex – part of the fetish world for example – and power. Exhibit A: The career women of the 80s.

”

Lauren Cochrane

Fashion writer and historian on the contested history of the stiletto, *The Ten: Stories Behind the Fashion Classics*, Lauren Cochrane, 2021

People say I am the king of painful shoes. I don't want to create painful shoes, but it is not my job to create something comfortable. I try to make high heels as comfortable as they can be, but my priority is design, beauty and sexiness. I'm not against them, but comfort is not my focus.

Christian Louboutin

On his shoes being notoriously difficult to wear, *British Vogue*, May 21, 2012

I do the summer collections in a hot place and the winter collections in a cold place.

”

Christian Louboutin

On his bi-annual collections and working with the seasons, *British Vogue*, April 5, 2018

How dare they imagine, if they have such respect for women, that any woman would do something she did not want to do? It's really degrading to women to think they are that stupid, that they do things according to rules made by feminists... it's an incredibly dated idea. No one is dictating the height of a heel. I don't put a gun to anyone's head.

”

Christian Louboutin

On the criticism received about his shoes and those who wear them, scotsman.com, May 8, 2012

But people ask me all the time, 'How can I walk in these heels?' I answer with the best compliment I remember that came from a woman who lives here in Paris. She said, 'Since I wore your shoes, Christian, I know Paris… I know my street much better. Heels permit me to take the time to look at the architecture of my street…

Now I take the time to look at things.' High heels give you time to think, to look at your surroundings – a camel has seen more in life than a very quick horse! Women should live to the rhythm of high-heeled shoes!

”

Christian Louboutin

On the benefits of wearing high-heeled shoes, *Vintage Shoes: Collecting Wearing Vintage Classics*, Caroline Cox, 2022

The first truly iconic Louboutin design to make its mark was the 2004 "Pigalle" Stiletto.

Named after the famously risqué Parisian neighbourhood, the "Pigalle" quickly became Louboutin's signature pump – sleek, sexy and undeniably timeless.

Its clean lines and sharp silhouette have made the shoe a mainstay of Louboutin's oeuvre since its inception, reimangined season after season while retaining its effortlessly seductive appeal.

[I want to] make a woman look sexy, beautiful, to make her legs look as long as I can.

”

Christian Louboutin

On creating heels that make legs appear elongated, businessoffashion.com, 2013

I did not think about it as a feeling. I thought about the structure, the gravity, the engineering of the shoe.

”

Christian Louboutin

On the "feeling" his shoes evoke, scotsman.com, May 8, 2012

“

He has sort of upped the ante in terms of how high the heel can soar.

”

Elizabeth Semmelhack

Senior Curator at the Bata Shoe Museum on the legacy of Louboutin, newyorker.com, March 21, 2011

I am always surprised by who wears my shoes. This is a good thing. There is no type of woman, but all my women like to feel feminine. They are women who are happy to be women.

Christian Louboutin

On the variety of customers who wear his shoes, scotsman.com, May 8, 2012

Following the success of the "Pigalle" came the next iconic design to solidify Louboutin's status as the foremost contemporary shoe designer – the "So Kate" pump, inspired by supermodel Kate Moss.

Launched in 2013, the "So Kate" shoe features a striking 12-centimetre heel, making it the tallest of Louboutin's signature styles. With its sharp silhouette and trademark "toe cleavage" detail, the design is equal parts daring and elegant.

Kate has a sharp style – simple and very complex at the same time. It sounded so much like Kate, simple yet very sophisticated. I felt this pump just had to be named after her, because it was so Kate.

”

Christian Louboutin

Speaking to *Vogue* about the inspiration behind the "So Kate" stiletto, *British Vogue*, May 7, 2024

“

The ‘So Kate’ shoe remains one of Louboutin’s most sought-after designs, beloved for its sleek shape and sky-high heel. Between 2019 and 2024 alone, over 300,000 pairs were sold globally – a testament to its enduring appeal and iconic status in the world of luxury footwear.

”

Elizabeth Semmelhack

Senior Curator at the Bata Shoe Museum on the legacy of Louboutin, newyorker.com, March 21, 2011

CHAPTER THREE

RED REIGN

STYLISH, LUXURIOUS, FLIRTATIOUS, SEDUCTIVE – THE RED SOLE OF A LOUBOUTIN HAS BEEN CALLED MANY THINGS OVER THE THREE DECADES SINCE ITS CREATION.

BORN FROM A HAPPY ACCIDENT, THE NOW-ICONIC RED SOLE HAS BECOME A LASTING SYMBOL OF GLAMOUR AND DESIRE – AND THERE IS NO DOUBT THAT IT WILL CONTINUE TO CAPTIVATE FOR YEARS TO COME.

If I had to go back and choose another colour, I would still choose red. If I have to stick to one as an identity, I will still keep my red.

”

Christian Louboutin

On the red sole being a reflection of his identity, dezeen.com, December 7, 2023

Pantone 18-1663 TPX

The iconic Pantone shade attributed to the Louboutin red sole.

Also known as Chinese Red, this colour is the brand's signature hue – so distinctive that it has been officially trademarked by Louboutin.

It was kind of a happy accident. I was at the factory in Italy, reviewing the first prototypes of the new collection. One was a Mary Jane high-heel. When turning the shoe, I noticed that there was a black sole, but that didn't match my sketch.

My assistant Sarah was next to me with a bottle of red nail polish, so I took it and coloured the sole with it. Suddenly, it was a revelation.

Christian Louboutin

On the birth of his famous red soles, ten-membership.com, March 5, 2021

In early 90s in France, there were a lot of women wearing black who claimed they did not like to wear colour. If you don't like colour, I thought, you might not wear green, but you will probably wear red on your nails, on your lips... That's why I decided to stick to red!

”

Christian Louboutin

On using the red sole to cater to ongoing fashion trends, eu.christianlouboutin.com

The colour red has long carried rich symbolism.

In the West, it evokes passion and seduction; in the East, it is a symbol of luck and prosperity.

Christian Louboutin draws on both interpretations, infusing his signature red sole with layers of meaning that transcend style alone.

The colour red is a representation of love, passion and life.

Christian Louboutin

On the symbolism behind the colour red, edition.cnn.com, November 20, 2023

Red is a transition. It's such an emotional colour, but also, it's not necessarily linked to colour. You may not like colours, but you still like red.

”

Christian Louboutin

On the enduring appeal of the colour red, dezeen.com, December 7, 2023

[Red is] strong, noticeable, powerful, and known for attracting good fortune.

”

Christian Louboutin

On the prosperity of the colour red, edition.cnn.com, November 20, 2023

The shiny red colour of the soles has no function other than to identify to the public that they are mine.

”

Christian Louboutin

On the purpose of the red sole, newyorker.com, March 21, 2011

Signifying love, passion and blood, red was used by Louboutin to create a visual shorthand to empower women, allowing them to break out of societal constraints while wearing his 'forbidden shoe'.

Darla-Jane Gilroy

Fashion historian on the significance of the red sole, *Little Book of Christian Louboutin: The story of the iconic shoe designer*, Darla-Jane Gilroy, 2021

I selected the colour because it is engaging, flirtatious, memorable, and the colour of passion.

Christian Louboutin

On why he chose red as his signature colour, newyorker.com, March 21, 2011

The red-lacquered sole is more than just a status symbol – it is a tribute to craftsmanship and artistic flair.

Maintaining the unmistakable flash of colour is no easy feat: over time the soles fade, and will need repainting to maintain their signature vibrancy.

While protective coatings are available, only the most trusted cobblers should touch the iconic red.

Nicole wore my shoes to Princess Diana's funeral. She was in black with little brown pumps – she has been wearing my shoes ever since.

”

Christian Louboutin

On Nicole Kidman wearing a pair of Louboutin shoes at Princess Diana's funeral in 1997, hollywoodreporter.com

The red sole was debuted in 1993, taking the fashion world by storm.

While it is difficult to pin the first fashionista to wear a red-bottom on the red carpet, early adopters included Nicole Kidman, who wore Louboutins to Princess Diana's funeral, and Elizabeth Taylor who wore a pair of Louboutins during Cannes Film Festival.

The idea of the shoes with the red soles has become symbolic of the luxury sensuous shoe.

”

Dr. Valerie Steele

Director and chief curator of the Museum at FIT, New York, on the Louboutin red sole, luxurydaily.com, September 3, 2019

I said, 'Doesn't it look matchy-matchy?' And she looked at me and said, 'I never had a problem with matchy-matchy.' I thought, who am I to say to one of the biggest stars ever that she looked matchy-matchy? I felt so stupid saying that to this huge icon.

Christian Louboutin

Recalling the time he worked with the iconic Elizabeth Taylor, footwearnews.com, July 17, 2020

"In 2003 the designer flew to Cannes and spent three days with Elizabeth Taylor, helping her to dress for the amfAR gala – in a look finished with a pair of green satin Louboutins. Since then, the appearance of those red soles at everything from film festivals to awards ceremonies and everything in between has been ubiquitous for decades."

Emma Sells

Fashion writer, on the explosion of the red-bottom-filled red carpet, marieclaire.co.uk, March 4, 2025

“The genius of Louboutin was to take this previously overlooked part of a shoe and make it not only visually dynamic but also commercially useful in communicating his brand.”

Darla-Jane Gilroy

Fashion historian on the brilliance of Louboutin, *Little book of Christian Louboutin: The story of the iconic shoe designer,* Darla-Jane Gilroy, 2021

A good shoe is the one which brings you joy when you think about it and when you wear it... Just like the glass slipper [from *Cinderella*] makes people dream, I try to make my shoes create the same effect, to allow you to be whatever character you dream to be.

”

Christian Louboutin

On designing shoes that have lasting effects, edition.cnn.com, November 20, 2023

The stiletto remains both a symbol of the patriarchy and also one of female empowerment.

”

Lauren Cochrane

Fashion writer, on the duality of the stiletto shoe, *The Ten: Stories Behind the Fashion Classics*, Lauren Cochrane, 2021

No interest. None. I never go clothes shopping, I have no patience for clothes.

Christian Louboutin

On his great love for shoes that triumphs clothes, *British Vogue*, April 5, 2018

I call Mr. Louboutin the greatest showman in footwear. To fans, the red sole equals the height of glamor.

”

Shannon Adducci

Footwear News style director on the legacy of Louboutin, edition.cnn.com, November 20, 2023

The shoe is very much an X-ray of social comportment.

”

Christian Louboutin

On the importance of the shoe, newyorker.com, March 21, 2011

The red sole has become a universal symbol of passion and allure – an association that Christian Louboutin fully embraces, both in his designs and in his bold statements.

The Pass mule is really the mistress shoe. It depends on the country, but the code is definitely leather, which is flesh.

Christian Louboutin

On the "Pass" mule, newyorker.com, March 21, 2011

I'd rather spend time with someone badly dressed but smart and funny and engaging than someone perfectly dressed and boring, who talks about clothes. To me, that's the image of a nightmare: A woman incredibly well-dressed, who can only talk about clothes. That kills it for me.

Christian Louboutin

On having conversations with substance and personality outside of fashion, *British Vogue*, April 5, 2018

The women I design shoes for are often comfortable with being themselves and embracing femininity.

”

Christian Louboutin

On encouraging self-confidence, ten-membership.com, March 5, 2021

“

There’s the promise of something wicked in Christian’s shoes. They’re a little dangerous, and there’s a sense of teetering on the precipice between avoiding dreary conventional good taste and tumbling into something far more outrageous.

”

Hamish Bowles

Vogue editor, on the genius of the Louboutin shoe, newyorker.com, March 21, 2011

There's no denying that Louboutin's red soles have become an enduring symbol of luxury, status and sensuality.

More than just a design choice, the signature red has transcended fashion trends for over three decades – weathering countless cultural shifts while continuing to embody bold femininity and unapologetic power.

You really need to be a criminal or a pervert to shock me.

”

Christian Louboutin

Known for his tongue-in-cheek one-liners, newyorker.com, March 21, 2011

Did you know that Christian Louboutin was once linked to a murder case? The designer received a call from police after his business card was found in a suspect's bag. The woman had no personal connection to Louboutin; she had simply picked up the card from one of his boutiques.

Ever the provocateur, Louboutin turned the bizarre incident into creative fuel, designing a pointed, strappy gold heel with a detachable sling – ideal, he joked, for a "Murderess".

CHAPTER FOUR

INNOVATION AND IMITATION

CHRISTIAN LOUBOUTIN IS ONE OF THE GREATEST FASHION INNOVATORS IN OUR TIME – EVEN TURNING HIS DESIGN EYE TO MENSWEAR AND CREATING A TRAINER LINE THAT'S COVETED BY "SNEAKERHEADS" ALL OVER THE WORLD.

BUT ALAS, WITH GREAT IDEAS COME IMITATORS, AND LOUBOUTIN HAS FOUND HIMSELF IN MORE THAN HIS FAIR SHARE OF COPYRIGHT COURT CASES.

Despite his reputation for razor-sharp heels, Louboutin hasn't shied away from stepping into new territories.

His trainer collections and expanding menswear line show that style and ease can go hand in hand – proving that his signature flair translates just as powerfully off the runway as it does on.

I started designing shoes for men when the singer Mika asked me to create a selection of pairs for his tour in 2009… He grew up surrounded by four sisters and a mother, and each time one of them wore a pair of my shoes, she felt empowered. And that's the feeling he wanted to embody when he was on stage.

”

Christian Louboutin

On the inception of the menswear line, ten-membership.com, March 5, 2021

I put myself in a specific state of mind to design a men's collection. For women, you're designing with curves in mind, while men's silhouettes require more angles.

Christian Louboutin

On the difference between designing for men and women, ten-membership.com, March 5, 2021

Renowned for leading trends rather than following them, Louboutin has been as influential in designing sneakers as his stiletto heels.

Darla-Jane Gilroy

Fashion historian on the impact Louboutin has had on the fashion trainer, *Little Book of Christian Louboutin: The story of the iconic shoe designer*, Darla-Jane Gilroy, 2021

The most important thing is that it looks good. That's the most important thing at the end of the day.

Christian Louboutin

On his priority when designing a shoe, dezeen.com, December 7, 2023

A shoe is not only a design, but it's a part of your body language, the way you walk.

Christian Louboutin

The shoe to Louboutin is so much more than the sum its parts, gq.com, September 20, 2012

I truly believe men should also be allowed to have the red sole!

Christian Louboutin

On making the red sole accessible for all, ten-membership.com, March 5, 2021

Men are like bulls. They cannot resist the red sole.

Christian Louboutin

On the appeal of the red sole for men, standard.co.uk, April 12, 2012

Louboutin first sought trademark protection of his signature red soles in 2001, but the application was initially rejected on the grounds that a sole was considered a basic, functional part of any shoe.

Undeterred, he persisted, and after his third attempt in 2008, Louboutin finally secured the trademark. It was officially recognized as "a lacquered red sole on footwear", cementing its place in fashion history.

Louboutin took a part of the shoe that had previously been ignored and made it not only visually interesting but commercially useful.

Elizabeth Semmelhack

Senior curator at the Bata Shoe Museum, Toronto, newyorker.com, March 21, 2011

You have to accept that ideas – like objects – cross ages and oceans, otherwise you isolate yourself.

”

Christian Louboutin

On the spread of fashion ideas, wwd.com, November 2, 2020

Sustainability comes back to respect.

”

Christian Louboutin

On his three-decade long tenure at the top of the luxury footwear industry, dezeen.com, December 7, 2023

As with any groundbreaking style, the Louboutin red-bottoms have inspired countless imitators over the years.

Since their debut, the striking soles have sparked not just trends, but also legal battles – with the signature style becoming one of the most litigated trademarks in fashion history.

But I have to stand up for who I am, and for everyone who believes there is still the possibility to start your own thing, instead of having to be paid and employed by just one or two possible groups.

Christian Louboutin

On his designs being imitated by larger luxury houses, *Independent*, May 26, 2012

The first major copyright battle for Louboutin came from a surprising source – Yves Saint Laurent, the fashion house where he had once worked.

When YSL released a red shoe that featured a red sole, Louboutin argued that it infringed on his now-iconic trademark. Following a high-profile legal clash that gripped the fashion world, the US Court of Appeals ruled in Louboutin's favour.

[YSL today] is totally apart from its fabulous and wonderful creator. He would never have done such a thing like that, for sure.

Christian Louboutin

Drawing a distinction between Yves Saint Laurent and the brand that continued after his death, *Independent*, May 26, 2012

[The case has] re-affirm[ed] the validity of our trademark rights on the red sole in the United States, an iconic signature of Christian Louboutin over the past 20 years.

”

Spokesperson for the Louboutin label upon the ruling in favour protecting the trademark of the red soles, *British Vogue*, October 16, 2012

We are delighted to note that Yves Saint Laurent have instead decided 'to refocus their energies on its business and creative designs'.

A Louboutin brand official statement on the result of the court case, ft.com, October 16, 2012

In 2018, Louboutin returned to the courts once again to defend the trademark of his iconic red sole – this time against the Dutch retailer vanHaren, which had begun selling red-soled shoes.

The European Court of Justice ultimately ruled in Louboutin's favour, validating the legal protection of the signature design.

For 26 years, the red sole has enabled the public to attribute the origin of the shoe to its creator, Christian Louboutin.

A spokesperson of Louboutin again reaffirms the originality of the red-bottomed design, theguardian.com, June 12, 2018

The sole is a point of silent recognition between women all over the world. Showing yours is a sort of flirtation.

Christian Louboutin

On the sisterhood of the red sole, thesun.ie, September 19, 2023

[The red sole] has provided an ingenious way to unify all of Louboutin's many brand extensions through a single colour that reflects his reputation for opulence, luxury, quality and sexuality.

Darla-Jane Gilroy

Fashion historian, on the significance of red to represent the Louboutin brand, *Little Book of Christian Louboutin: The story of the iconic shoe designer*, Darla-Jane Gilroy, 2021

Quality is always vital as you'll want to keep the shoes for as long as possible. But more than anything, you have to pick a style that makes you feel happy, strong and reflects the mood you want to be in.

”

Christian Louboutin

On finding a balance between quality and happiness, ten-membership.com, March 5, 2021

[My company] has been built on the same principles of trust and freedom.

Christian Louboutin

On the values of his brand, BBC, March 2, 2020

CHAPTER FIVE

A CULTURAL PHENOMENON

FROM PRINCESSES TO POP STARS, RAPPERS TO POLITICIANS AND ACTORS TO A-LISTERS, LOUBOUTINS HAVE GRACED THE FEET OF SOME OF THE MOST RECOGNIZABLE FIGURES IN POP CULTURE.

WHETHER STRUTTING ACROSS THE SET OF *SEX AND THE CITY* OR NAME-DROPPED IN CHART-TOPPING HITS, THESE ICONIC HEELS HAVE LEFT AN UNMISTAKABLE STAMP ON THE WORLD OF FASHION AND BEYOND.

Madonna is a feminist and has been doing more for the cause than all the grumpy feminists, who are giving nothing back by being grumpy.

”

Christian Louboutin

On Madonna and feminism, *Independent*, May 26, 2012

Since bursting onto the scene in the 1990s, Christian Louboutin's heels have become a pop-culture staple – featured on red carpets, poular songs, and TV and movie screens.

From collaborations with Taylor Swift for her "Eras" tour to being name-dropped in the lyrics of Cardi B's songs, Louboutin remains a symbol of aspiration, ever in the spotlight.

Marlene [Dietrich] represents elegance and posture. She is the master of knowing how to cross the legs, how to arch the step. The front of the shoe has to represent Marlene's sense of character. Then there is the way you walk in it…

It's symbolized by the back of a woman and who better represents that than Marilyn? Think of the first time we see her in *Some Like It Hot*, walking away... It's a perfect example of how a... shoe tells you how to walk.

”

Christian Louboutin

On his silver screen inspiration, scotsman.com, May 8, 2012

“[Louboutin] opened his first shop in 1991 and Princess Caroline of Monaco was his first customer, closely followed by Diane von Furstenberg, Catherine Deneuve and many, many more.”

Emma Sells

Fashion writer, on the instant love that the rich and famous found for Louboutin's designs, marieclaire.co.uk, March 4, 2025

Since the opening of his first boutique, Christian Louboutin's creations have drawn a loyal following among celebrities and A-listers alike.

From princesses to popstars and actresses to supermodels, many famous feet have donned a red sole.

It is exciting to work with someone who has such a strong aesthetic and character… Getting to know Angelina through a fun collaboration has been one of my greatest pleasures.

”

Christian Louboutin

On working with Angelina Jolie, harperbazaar.com, August 8, 2014

I loved working with Miss Piggy – she never once told me that my shoes were uncomfortable!

Christian Louboutin

On making custom puppet shoes for the Miss Piggy's appearance on *Late Night with Jimmy Fallon* in 2011, hollywoodreporter.com

Louboutin's first breakthrough on the small screen came courtesy of the cult hit *Sex and the City*, where shoes were arguably the true loves of the protagonists' lives. Unlike most of the wardrobe – largely gifted by designers – Louboutins had to be purchased by the costume department. At the time, Louboutin couldn't imagine just how impactful the show's spotlight would be, unaware that his red soles were about to be viewed by millions.

The stiletto's role in *Sex and the City* subscribes to a particular type of 'because you're worth it' commodity feminism popular around the millennium. The fact that women were buying designer stilettos for themselves was read as the ultimate in independence, emancipation and empowerment.

”

Lauren Cochrane

Fashion historian, on the significance of the red sole in *Sex and the City*, *The Ten: Stories Behind the Fashion Classics*, Lauren Cochrane, 2021

Yes, I know. They called me but they don't want to pay. Nothing is great publicity when it doesn't pay. That's my job. I design shoes and people buy them.

Christian Louboutin

On refusing to give the costume department of *Sex and the City* free pairs of his shoes, refinery29.com, May 20, 2017

Pat and I chose to do one of each. Perhaps because both were so delicious in colour and seemed in harmony with the dress but also because we simply loved doing one of each.

”

Sarah Jessica-Parker

Actress, on her iconic mismatched Louboutin moment in *Sex and the City*, vogue.com, June 26, 2019

You're dying to have this thing or that thing? That's an important feeling that everybody should be able to have, regardless of how famous you are… That said, I give shoes to friends – so if you're a friend, celebrity or not, I give shoes. But I'm not saying all stars are good friends of mine.

Christian Louboutin

On not giving away his shoes for free, refinery29.com, May 20, 2017

I'm not the type of designer to put up an Instagram with my new BFF, who happens to be a big star. I never did, I never will.

Christian Louboutin

On letting his designs take the spotlight, *British Vogue*, April 5, 2018

You put on a pair of Louboutins and the world changes colour.

”

Rossy de Palma

Actress and model, on the effect of Louboutin shoes, azquotes.com

It started when she was 14, and I remember she had these 'So Kates' on... It's the first time she'd ever worn them... And she's like, 'I have to take these shoes off.' I'm like, 'You will not take these shoes off.' And she kept them on, and the next day, and the next...

Christian Louboutin

Zendaya's stylist, on why Zendaya always wears 'So Kate' shoes, harperbazaar.com, May 10, 2024

Really good taste, you have to forget about it.

Christian Louboutin

As seen on newyorker.com, March 21, 2011

When designing a bespoke pair of shoes, Christian Louboutin creates a wax mould of the client's feet.

Visitors to his atelier often remark on its slightly surreal atmosphere – walls lined with thousands of pairs of wax feet hanging on the walls, many marked with the world's most recognizable names.

I feel like a designer, and also like a doctor. As you probably know, a doctor has secrets, and a doctor never speaks of his patients. When I do things that are public for my patient around a movie, I would easily discuss it. But otherwise, I do not discuss my patient-slash-client, as a good doctor should.

Christian Louboutin

On client confidentiality, standard.co.uk, August 11, 2015

“

My wardrobe is brimming with Louboutins – the classic black Pigalle stiletto in patent or matte black leather is my go-to shoe. I have so many pairs that Christian designed a style with a sharper toe and nail-thin heel, which he named the ‘So Kate’.

”

Kate Moss

On her collection of Louboutin shoes, edition.cnn.com, November 20, 2023

My favourite sound is definitely mules. If it was an instrument, it's really ping – the touch of the black keys of the piano.

Christian Louboutin

Often referring to the sounds that his shoes make, newyorker.com, March 21, 2011

I once turned down a well-paying ad campaign for a major luxury shoe brand because I have such loyalty to him [Louboutin] both as a designer and friend!

Dita Von Teese

Burlesque dancer and Louboutin muse on rejecting rival campaign offers, hollywoodreporter.com, January 20, 2015

Louboutins are crafted not only for catwalks, but also for the spotlight.

Designed to dazzle on stage as well as off, they have become the footwear of choice for powerhouse performers like Beyoncé and Taylor Swift, who regularly incorporate the brand into their tour wardrobes

When I make dancing shoes for Beyoncé, I think of Elizabeth II at her coronation – the Queen's cobbler was told that if there was a problem with the shoe it wasn't the fall of the person, but the fall of the monarchy. I take it very seriously.

Christian Louboutin

On designing shoes for Beyoncé's 2016 Superbowl performance, hollywoodreporter.com, 2025

The [Eras Tour] stage clothes were instrumental in the overall inspiration. It has been a pleasure for someone like me, who started designing shoes for cabaret dancers, to imagine pairs for her tour and thinking about the overall performance and how the shoes will come to life.

”

Christian Louboutin

On designing shoes for Taylor Swift to wear during the "Eras" tour – the highest grossing tour of all time, instyle.com, November 27, 2024

We have worked with Taylor for a while, since the 2010s, on music videos, different things, red carpets, et cetera... Then we worked together for her 'Reputation' tour, which was 2018. So, it really felt natural to design pairs for the tour, encompassing all of the eras.

Christian Louboutin

On working with Taylor Swift throughout her career, instyle.com, November 27, 2024

Each pair is crafted with a signature red rubber sole, which makes it easy to dance. We typically incorporate this feature for musicians' tours to withstand the performances night after night.

Christian Louboutin

On the differences between designing for stage and red carpet, instyle.com, November 27, 2024

When the show opened, all I could see was scaffolding on the stage and I thought, 'Oh, my God, she's going to climb on the scaffolding and jump from it'. I was paralyzed. I couldn't enjoy the show as I was so worried about her breaking her neck. I knew the height of the heel.

Christian Louboutin

Remembering the late Tina Turner, another signer who tore up the stage, and her ability to perform in his stilettos, thesun.ie, September 19, 2023

Kate Moss is not the only A-lister to have a Louboutin design named in her honour. In 2011, Louboutin announced the "Blake", a tribute to actress and longtime friend Blake Lively.

More recently, speculation has swirled around the 2025 Miss Z shoe – rumoured to be inspired by Zendaya – though the designer has yet to confirm these suspicions.

“I also like to dress up… I also think that’s relaxing – to put on a great pair of Louboutins.”

Blake Lively

Actress, claiming that wearing Louboutins relaxes her, glamour.com, June 30, 2016

CHAPTER SIX

LIFE BY LOUBOUTIN

STEP INTO YOUR
BEST LIFE WITH THESE
WORDS OF WISDOM
BY THE
GRANDMASTER OF
SHOE DESIGN.

I do things for; I never do things against. That's my motto.

Christian Louboutin

On his design ethos, *10 Magazine*, December 15, 2021

High heels empower a woman in a way. The woman carries her clothes, but her shoes carry the woman.

Christian Louboutin

On how shoes can empower the wearer, thesun.ie, September 19, 2023

I don't have long-term projects – I follow my instincts and I'm open to opportunities. My plan is to see what comes next…

Christian Louboutin

On the future of his career, elledecoration.co.uk, April 9, 2020

[The] philosophy of 'luck is an attitude' is similar to my own motto: 'Why not?'

Christian Louboutin

On his life philosophy, *Independent*, May 26, 2012

I'm not obsessed with doing something first.

”

Christian Louboutin

Although Louboutin did not invent the stiletto, he is credited with taking the shoe to new heights, *Vintage Shoes: Collecting Wearing Vintage Classics*, Caroline Cox, 2022

I think I make a very useless work and I'm very proud of it.

Christian Louboutin

On being proud of his creations, regardless of their use, theguardian.com, August 12, 2015

“

I’m thinking if everything goes wrong and I have to live in that place for the rest of my life, where do I put the kitchen? Where do I put the tables? Because one thing I know how to do is make crêpes. So, I’m always thinking, if everything goes wrong, I’ll transform the place into a crêpe restaurant.

”

Christian Louboutin

On his back-up plan for his house, *10 Magazine*, December 15, 2021

To prefer to show the beautiful side of the world, it's a choice, and I love that choice. I love that choice to fight with beauty, instead of fighting with violence, with anger. You know, I think that beauty is a great tool.

”

Christian Louboutin

On the importance and power of beauty, *10 Magazine*, December 15, 2021

Probably a little naughty myself, so I just gave that to my shoes.

”

Christian Louboutin

On his cheeky style as a reflection of his personality, *Christian Louboutin: The World's Most Luxurious Shoes*, Channel 4, 2009

When you do something that you love, even if it doesn't work, even if it's useless, as long as you have pleasure doing it and it pleases you, you will have never wasted your time.

Christian Louboutin

On spending time doing what you love, dezeen.com, December 7, 2023

Christian Louboutin's creations transcend footwear – blending art, fantasy and empowerment.

His iconic red soles have left an undeniable mark on fashion and culture, symbolizing confidence and allure.

With no sign of the maestro slowing down, the red-bottoms will undoubtedly continue to dominate fashion and popular culture for years to come.

A good shoe is a shoe which makes you feel good, look good, feel confident, engaged, and fierce.

Christian Louboutin

On how shoes should make you feel, edition.cnn.com, November 20, 2023

We have a phrase in French, *le petit quelque chose qui fout tout par terre*, which means 'the little thing that f**ks everything up.'

99

Christian Louboutin

On imperfect design, newyorker.com, March 21, 2011

I am not producing pills to cure people, so I feel that the whole system should be slightly joyful.

Christian Louboutin

On the importance of joy in his work, newyorker.com, March 21, 2011

The secret to good design – and it's a very basic answer – is to be true to yourself.

Christian Louboutin

On how to create an iconic design, dezeen.com, December 7, 2023